MW00939374

"I AM" Messages to Humanity

Guidance on How to Lift in Vibration and Embrace Your Human Experience

A healing journey out of fear and into LOVE

Copyright 2018 Deanna Avakumova (Shanti)

ISBN-13:978-1718875135

I am here not to fit into the common, I am here to create a new normal.

My story is the story of amazing growth and transformation, my story is the story of forgiveness and faith, my story is the story of learning to love and learning to self-love, my story is the story of watching heartache and surrendering to the truth, my story is the story of overcoming and transformational healing, my story is the story of returning home without dying.

My story is your story!

Welcome to the sacred space, the space between you and your heart space, the space of pure unconditional love that flows all abound, limitless and all encompassing. These words as they speak out to you from these pages will activate in you the most sacred aspect of you, your pure innocence, your true essence, your "I AM." It is here with the purpose to further your awakening and deepen your connection with your "I AM," with your heart-centered consciousness.

Each word vibrating with the frequency of love will assist you in consciously aligning with the same. As you digest each word, process its vibration as it settles into each cell of your physical form, you will feel renewed, realigned and repositioned into the light.

Each message-conversation is purposely delivered to awaken you, to activate your light codes, to activate LOVE within you.

Some conversations are one line long and those are to be pondered upon the most.

I trust you will enjoy these messages, as much as I have in receiving them, and will benefit from them. I have learned a lot in the process of these transmissions, which took place from 2016 – 2017.

Remember, you are a magnificent creation, you are a masterful co-creator of your realities and all others. Let us embark together on this miraculous journey of transformation, transmuting all that no longer serves our highest good.

Embracing our light and our shadow and as we embrace it, all the shadow turns to light.

My commitment to staying true to the callings of my heart has been rooted in me since birth and it took years to suppress it and then years to regain it.

Our fundamental realizations define who WE are. Mine are rooted in the fact that I am not a body, but rather a spirit in the body walking this beautiful earth, seeing, feeling, smelling, touching, perceiving with all of my senses in a tangible kind of way.

Regardless of how much I perceive or sense, it is only in the moments of deep silence and mere breathing that I come to a place of complete peace, serenity, joyful bliss and fulfillment and in full union with the divinity that resides within my body.

You are a *supreme spiritual creation*, awaken into the truth.

Why do we keep coming here to this density and this dimension and this reality so we can climb out of the circle that we keep going around called karma? For each corrected wrong-doing, we do more wrong over and over again slowing down our process of climbing upward toward reunion with the source. This mess we are in is called Free Will and enjoying the pleasures of this world bypassing fulfillment as we get caught up in satisfaction! Source doesn't interfere, it allows us, its children, to make our mistakes and learn from them. It is these countless lifetimes that allow just that and so much more: lifetime after lifetime, baby step by baby step, we get closer to the truth that has always remained and dwelled and burned like eternal fire within us as the spark of light in the darkness of amnesia!

We must resist being sucked into the density! We must rise above the human challenge! It is a most challenging task we keep coming here to master!

Once we overcome it, we become masterful! We get to go home because we chose to step into love. Because where there is love, there is no negative karma! We get to become one with source again! Homecoming at its most precious essence of all- LOVE.

The chaos and the absence of love right now on our planet is showing up to show us to which level, we as humanity, have sunk and what it will take to climb up the evolutionary ladder!

The solution and way out are within us. It is called love! It is truly love that can save us all! If we all stepped into it, if we all connected with the Source, with our creator, with our soul!

So, let us rise above the chaos in the world and dive deep into the light of love within each of us!

Blessings be,

SHANTI

"I AM" SPEAKS

"Grace is always greater than any mistake"

There is a place where you can go, where mercy lives. It is a place where you feel your heartbeat. In this place you hold on to pure love.

This is the place where I shall meet you.

Dwell in the greatness of your own presence, and when WE say presence, WE mean the most authentic aspect of your being, that part of you whose voice is so loud that for some of you it takes a lifetime to suppress and then a lifetime to awaken.

Listen to the voice that arises from within, from the deepest and the lightest. Let it come up flowing freely as you make way for its rupture into the present moment in the here and now.

WE speak to you from eternity, from the place of where no aspect of your being goes unnoticed from the place where you are free, boundless and eternal.

You are so loved dear one.

Upgrade your Vibration: Show your divinity that is dwelling in your humanity and present it to the world in here and now!

In the unity of it all, you stand apart in your uniqueness and your ability to connect and merge with the prime creation with the source of all that there is. May this uniqueness be recognized only in the face of love and light for the highest and greatest good of all!

You are present here at this point in time, to be part of Ascension and awakening of the Human race! You are powerful beings who can create with your hands and your minds.

Root yourselves in the name of your divinity, in compassion of your hearts and in the faith that as you commit to becoming LOVE and start greeting all with LOVE, then old will crumble away, and a new Human will emerge through you, the one that is LOVE itself and dwells in LOVE at all times. You came into the world of contrast, where fear is the opposite of LOVE so you can get to know what LOVE is. And with that knowing and recognition of LOVE, you cannot un-know it.

The density of your physical experience kept you captive for too long, time to break out of your shell and into the truthful purpose of your experience which lies in realization of the greater outside forces that are of equal magnitude within you. We once again speaking of your spirit, speaking of your inner voice that is the "spokesman" for your inner being that is in full alignment with the source of all that there is, with the prime creator of which you are a great part of. Live your life knowing who you are in essence, know that it is YOU who have chosen your path, and it is YOU who is capable of great change, but that change must start with you. It must start with simple and kind act toward yourself – LOVE.

Love yourself the way you love little children, allow yourself to send love to yourself, allow yourself to send love to all the aspects of yourself the good and the ugly, the smart and the dummy and know dear one that we pick these words to deliver the message to you to deliver the message that you are to love all of yourself for all your perfect imperfections, for all that you did not want to do but did it, for all that you did not want to say but said it, for all for which you are sorry, love that about yourself. And once you establish that kind of unconditional love for yourself, then dear one, you are ready for the world to love you back.

Out of silence and into devotion.

Out of the silence and into the LOVE.

Dear one, when you are at the fork, choose what feels warm and fulfilling to you, that dear one is your choice. Make your choices that fills your being with joy, make the kind of choices that inspire you, make choices that you feel as if you are at flight. Spread your "wings" soar high and not cling to your nest. You see, dear one, your nest is your safety and the sky is your home. Finding balance is of essence to your wellbeing here in your physical world of duality and contrast. Lift, fly, float, soar into your true inspirations and as you align with your own truth and as you stay in your integrity wellbeing, fulfillment your innate ability to be miraculous will just be! You, dear one, always and always and always LOVED.

Infinite potential you are. That's what we tell you. You are beings capable of much creation and much destruction. And yet as we observe your free will zone, we observe with joy and without judgements. Your free will is your most precious gift that you can utilize with the purpose of aligning with the light or the with the purpose of aligning of the absence of the light.

You see, dear one, we see all as light. All is perfect as it is in the eyes of the creator. For your human experience this presents a challenge; for the mind places judgements as living in the contrast based dense reality, you step outside of your alignment with the absolute truth of who you are in essence. You step outside of deep realization, belief and absolute truth that you carry within an enormous potential that goes unrealized simply because of your choices. Potential of which we speak of lies in your own power of creation: your daily reality, your dreams, your life path is of your own doing and creation. But as the deep ingrained understanding of the opposite belief- that you are not powerful enough to create your world - sets limitations and more densities into already dense reality that you are in.

You see, dear one, a much greater part of you is here with us, in the non-physical. You are us. And we are you. That part of you is us is pure infinite potential is pure bliss, consciousness and joy. It is now your call to find the power within you to stand in your own power of your own creation. To realize how special, you all are without any single exception regardless of what you heard or were told before. It is you who holds the power to stand in your own alignment and be unbendable to the forces of doubt outside of you. We are here always with you and always will continue reminding you and calling you into stepping into your true eternal essence, into your true infinite wisdom, into your absolute truth. You are who you make it to be. You are powerful creator. You create with your intent, mind and hands... So, we say to you - believe! Be masterful in your creations. Believe that what you think what you desire what you say and what you do becomes your path. Make it the one of light, joy, bliss, gratitude, admiration and appreciation for your eternal truth is always within you and available to you. You must want to access that truth and through that genuine desire to live out your truth you come in alignment with the higher aspects of yourselves, with us, with all that there is. We love you so.

Beloved child of light and love, we are surrounding you with the waves of invisible veil, the veil that carries the highest frequency, the frequency of your awakening and self-realization into the loving nurturing and divine human that you are. You have come here into this dimension for self-realization and manifestation of all of your potential; each moment of inspiration is a precious gift and not to be ignored, for your daily inspirations, those fleeting moments are your callings of your true YOU. Your true mission that is to be accomplished and realized. Do not focus on all that serves as a barrier between you and your divinely inspired callings of the heart. The amount of support that is available to you is not quantifiable - it is immense, it is as vast as the universe, and it supports you in all of your endeavors.

We are always here and you are so loved. We are you.

Do tell your heart "to beat again," when it feels like it just can't go on any more. Make that stand before yourself and listen to every beat of your divine center of your connection with the highest aspects of yourself. It is calling you to stand in your own light to face the challenges of your own density and the density of the dimension of limitations.

Everyone you know and do not know, seeks love that is never failing, and yet it has always been within you. It is why you are here, beloved one, learning to see all with the eyes of love, compassion and humility. Learn to become that, which you already are.

You are not who you were a second ago, you are always becoming, surrender your defenses, submit to LOVE.

When you find purpose in whatever it is that feels right for you, follow it, dear one, and do not let the density of the physical experience stop you from expressing your truth. Or stop you from stepping into your full expression of the source that you are. Do not allow the limitations of your perception of your reality prevent you from allowing your own unfolding.

Know that you are GOD experiencing itself.

The "down the road good" can only surface from the goodness in now.

Whatever it is, it is not worthy of your judgement and heartache... it is only worthy of your LOVE.

Whatever it is that is coming AT you, it is here FOR you. You are simply to love it. You might say, how I can LOVE something that hurts so much, and WE say, because you CAN.

It is a CHOICE. FREE WILL CHOICE. Send love and light to all that hurts you. Thus, transmuting it fully, each time you do it.

This does not mean stay where it hurts and allow any disrespect to your being. It simply means, recognizing that it is here to serve you, to show you what is yet to be learned and recognized and be transmuted and transformed. That is the reason for the TIME that exists here in this reality that is the reason for your being here - to TRANSFORM while in human form, for transformation is a natural process of life, death and rebirth.

Thus, is Christ Consciousness. This is awakening! This is expanded consciousness.

It is your choice if you choose to cross into higher dimensions into higher states of consciousness into your own AWAKENING into the TRUTH of your eternal loving nature.

Don't let the chains of yesterday bind you so tight that you can't breathe freely, so tightly that you simply can't inhale LOVE anymore.

See yourself as free and boundless, that is your true nature.

You are nothing less than AMAZING.

You are nothing less than LOVE.

You are a Divine Human birthing its way through the challenges of your human experience.

You are so loved, dear one.

Forgiveness is a grand gesture in a display of your affection for Prime Creator – Source.

It is in this journey that you are transcending limitations of your duality via the path of love. It starts with you, within you. This is return to your innocence, return to your essence. This is the way to lift your physical self in vibration. This is transformation. *This is transforming the transcended.*

Forgive yourself, and all else.

Now is the moment for you to become a fearless lover of love. Step into the Love vibration.

Greetings beloved one. We are here. As humanity you must stand as one to make it through the times of change. The change is here it is inevitable and it is up to you how you withstand the change, the shift, the shift that takes you closer to the light, to the source of the creation of all that there is. We are assisting you now with the symptoms that you as humanity and individuals are experiencing, and these symptoms are just signs of how much density is to be released before you can move into the light and accept and integrate the higher frequency waves and assimilate them. We brought various technologies and will continue to be doing so to facilitate that for you and others, but not everyone is ready for it, not everyone will welcome it, not everyone will understand it, but those who are guided and feel called on it, those are the ones who are ready to receive and transform and cross over to the higher realms of consciousness.

QUESTION: How can I and other lightworkers get those who are not responding to the call to change?

ANSWER: That is their free will. You cannot go against free will, dear one, therefore their actions will bring them what they are on course for. And not what you want them to be on the course for. You can try dear one, but you cannot breach the free will zone. But you can be the one to inspire the change. And we are here every step of the way supporting you and all of humanity in this massive endeavor of Ascending into the highest states of consciousness available for all. But it takes your commitment and free will to move into that direction.

Our beloved, mercy, love and peace are awaiting YOU on the other side! That other side is within you. Unlock your divine potential, build a bridge of golden light linking all of you, uniting all your being in its full glory from all directions of time fully cleared from any negativity, any obstacles that hold you and prevent you from your own Ascension into the divine human that you are.

We are the aspect of you ascended into the highest realms in alignment with the divine with love and light calling you to join in on our great endeavors to awaken you. Join us in celebration of your divine nature in joy!

Greetings dear one. We are here surrounding you with the light and love as you connect with the essence of all existence, which is love.

Today we are wanting to share with you the love that we have for you and when we say you, we mean you as a whole, as humanity manifested in a single unit of love in the form you call Shanti. Before your eyes now lays an ocean covering your beloved planet which is in great deal of pain, that is the best way we can deliver by words what we mean and what your planet earth is feeling at this moment.

We are not saying this to instill guilt in you we are saying this promote a shift, a change in you and in the way you lead your lives. Consumed by worries of your mind and densities of your own thoughts and ambitions which take you out of the balance of equilibrium that is essential for successful transition into higher realms. That balance is essential to be maintained at all times. You swing like pendulums from one edge to another and for brief moments you come to center as in meditation or napping or just slowing down.

Today our message for you, dear one, as you spread this word of light: slow down. Breathe. Look around yourselves with your eyes closed. Just the way you do and feel when you kiss your loved one. In that moment all comes to a perfect stillness and all you feel in that moment is peace and serenity of your own innocence. This is what we are calling you for, to live your life from that point always in all that you do and in all that you think.

Any thoughts or words that are born out of that moment of stillness, connection, oneness with the harmony and flow of life, all will be of light for in that moment you are rooted in love and cultivating love. You become a love generating physical vessel as opposed to the one who generates worrisome thoughts of whatever it might be or whatever it is you fear.

Look in front of you, Shanti, this is love. Like the ocean and the waves caress the rocks on the shores, so you shall caress the spirit of the reader with these words. We love you so, and for now we are complete.

Love and live in your I am presence, dwell in your God presence and allow the downpour of the crystalline white light to come down and surround you, lift you in vibration, envelope you and bring you closer to your divine human.

If being the light of the world seems like a challenge to you in the here and now moment, then start by being the light in your own world and in the darkest of moments remember who you truly are, a child of light.

Choose to accept what is and only see the light in it all, learn to see the silver lining, learn to see the good in it. Learn to count your blessings every day and focus on them.

Choose to think conscious thoughts, choose to be the child of light, and choose to manifest LIGHT, LOVE, PEACE and HARMONY.

CHOOSE LOVE!

All suffering is here not to happen "to" you, there is no malicious plan conspired against you, everything is here happening "for" you, for your own growth and evolution, everything here simply is being of your service, but you must recognize that through such an awareness! By stepping into such an awareness, you go beyond matter.

By going into such state of consciousness, realization and deep-rooted understanding that all is happening and is of your choosing you can establish a platform of gratitude for all that there is and from this platform of acceptance and gratitude your welcome transformation. The kind of transformation that puts you into a state of overall well-being, harmonious living and alignment.

When all falls away, breathe and rest at the feet of the divine and all shall become Vivid!

In the times of the greatest despair it takes a great skill and commitment to stay aligned with the light source at all times. What do we mean when we say stay aligned with source? We mean for you to focus on your wellbeing a place where despair is absent. By focusing on the despair, by focusing on what you perceive as a problem, you only perpetuate its existence and continued manifestation and persistence.

We are not telling you to dwell in your problem and not take steps in climbing out of where you don't want to be, we are telling to focus solely on where you want to be, that is your solution. Focus on your goal, take steps necessary toward it by listening to the guidance of your own heart. And as you stay focused on solutions, do not give a second of your attention to your problem of which you are seeking relief from.

You see, dear, your inability to focus on the bigger picture and what is yet to come and your extremely well practiced skill on focusing what is right before you, what seems as your reality and it is your physical reality is what keeps you stuck in that manifestation and attracting more of the same . We tell you, have faith and by faith we mean know that wellbeing is what is meant for you and only you can get in the way of it if you continue giving your undivided attention to the situations you are not wanting to be part of!

Our answer to you will always be: to align with your wellbeing regardless of your physical reality and let physical reality reflect your inner state of wellbeing. This is what you have come here to practice and perfect. Perfecting the skill of mastery of becoming a masterful creator of new reality of new earth where wellbeing is its vibration in physical and nonphysical. Thus, is the building blocks of new earth.

When you taste the sweetest love of the prime creator and feel its glow and flow from your whole being, you are home dear one!

The greatest miracle is being able to speak your truth at all times maintaining your integrity to your true identity, to your own divine truth that dwells in your heart space. Let all the illusions about expectations fall away as you speak the words infused with the light of the TRUTH.

Love and live in your "I am", dwell in your God presence and allow the downpour of the crystalline white light come down surround you lift you in vibration envelop you and bring you closer to your divine human. If being the light of the world seems like a challenge to you now, then start by being the light in your own world, in your immediate surroundings and situations and events, and in the darkest of moments, please remember who you truly are, which is a child of light. Choose to accept what is and only see the light in it all, learn to see the silver lining, learn to see the good in it. Learn to count your blessings every day. Choose to think good thoughts, choose to be the child of light that you are, choose to manifest LIGHT, LOVE AND PEACE, HARMONY at all times.

What is your choice?

The knowing that you have within is beyond all doubt or belief.

How often do you get curious about yourself, and how often do you judge yourself? Look within with curiosity, not judgement. Curiosity about who you truly are, what are your true passions and desires? Explore, marvel, act on it!

Your soul is calling!

Awakening is not some sort of final destination at which you arrive and you get off the ride. Awakening is your opportunity to start anew and fresh, but this time from the place of full alignment with your highest wisdom available to you from the place of constant deliberate awareness presence. A place where you are rooted in gratitude and knowing that you are the creator of your reality and that there is so much more to your duality - its a place of restart renewal rejuvenation and launching into your own momentum of realization that you are a powerful spiritual divine being - pure consciousness - manifested in your physical vessel for the purpose of CO-creation.

When you start to care less about what people think about you, you become free, and when you are free, you are home, dear one.

Go for unbelievable, launch for impossible, why place a cap to your potential. When all you have around you is potential! Choose the path of unfolding. How? By not resisting what is there laid out before you. You are living in the midst of great changes, so the best way to navigating through these changes is by learning to adapt and detach from the ways of your comfort zone. Everything is changing, your attachment to constancy and permanency is the resistance, liberate yourself from attachment to "how you did it" and focus on how to do it in NOW. And as you navigate the seas of change, know that you are the captain of this ship and it is you who are steering its direction on the path of least resistance. Allowing the unfolding.

On raising children: bear witness to their own unfolding, gently guiding them without imposing your ways of being onto them. Guide them the way divine gently guides you without imposing or breaching your free will. Become the space for their unfolding as you steer them into the direction of their choosing.

Speaking from the heart, is one true language, one tongue that is yet is to be fully mastered by humanity as a whole. Many here on this planet are awakening into it. This is the language that does not require thinking that does not require much effort, this is language that is effortless, it is ever flowing at all times. All that is needed is to simply breathe into it and "let the words fall out."

You know you are lifting and raising your vibrational frequency and improving your alignment when you find yourself more and more out of the state of thinking thoughts that are rooted in fear and doubt! And you see yourself being enthusiastic about creating and thinking your thoughts consciously at all times in alignment with joy, bliss, hope, faith, happiness – LIGHT. You see your thoughts are what mostly define your vibrational state of being. Lighter and brighter thoughts – lighter and brighter you. It starts with a thought and it ends with your reality. Look at your reality from the point of view of the observer and if what you see is not of your liking then start paying close attention to the quality of your thoughts. Thought, word, deed.

Humanity's strength lies in the power of the light within ONE.

Yes, we tell you this to remind you of your natural composition. As you contemplate this concept, further alignment and shifting within your consciousness occurs lifting you higher and higher.

Take time, sink into the silence, feel and see light within you, pouring down upon you and all around you. Align with the brilliance of the light abound all around, for as within, so is without. You are all part of the greater ONE. Take responsibility, take charge, take command, take on mastery of your own thoughts and direct them into aligning with the highest vibration that there is, which PEACE AND LOVE is.

Love yourself in the most intimate of ways. Intimate- for only you know your struggles, only you know the real pain you have endured and only YOU know how to truly LOVE YOURSELF. Through all of your struggles and pain, you have never been separate from your HIGHEST SELF, so only YOU can set a true INTENT to find your way back to your SELF.

As you set your intent...I as "I AM," shall meet you there.

Anchor your light in here and now.

Walk through the doorways of your center, departing the place of conditions, judgments and assumptions of your mind.

Be LOVE and know that you are so LOVED.

Do not be the obstacle to your own wellbeing!

You start your life over every minute. Every minute of your day is your golden opportunity to take a leap of faith and knowing that you can start it over right now right here, you can start from the ground zero: where you are rooted in gratitude only.

Gratitude for what is, regardless of "what is" look like or feels like to you or to others. And aim and focus on what you want your "what is" to be. If someone is sick, focus on their well-being, and when you are praying for them, do not pray out of desperation to save them, pray out of gratitude for what is, for what is -is the experience you came here for. And as you find yourself dwelling in the state of gratitude during the day, notice and see how the day unfolds in that same frequency for you.

Pushing and trying harder and harder, by pushing harder, it moves less. Relax into your own unfolding, bless all and everyone, love yourself the way you never did, ignore what is not giving you joy bliss and happiness and focus on what does, even if that is not yet in your physical realm, but know that it is very much in the energetic and awaiting your alignment with it, so it can manifest fully into your physical reality.

Know what you want, be clear in your wishes and dreams and desires, AND FOCUS on that and let it all unfold before you, do not be the obstacle to your own wellbeing!

Be grateful, be only grateful for all is working out always for your highest and greatest good. And do not resist. Do not resist what is surfacing, do not resist what is happening, do not resist all that you do not want. For what you resist does persist. So the way out of this continuous resistance is to find a path where you are resisting the least by loving and blessing all that has caused you pain! That is transforming and transmuting into light.

A word of advice: If someone lashes out at you, do not see an enemy in them, but only choose to see a heart in need of healing, choose to see unconsciousness that is here to awaken you. Choose LOVE at all times so you can spread love in all directions of time, dear one.

Look at life the way it sees YOU.

Collect the acts of kindness ONLY to give them away.

You are forever!

Surrender your decision-making to your HEART.

Give LOVE permission to make all the choices on your behalf.

There is no going wrong when you make your decisions with your heart and allow your emotions and feelings about your own decision guide you. Do not think or overthink. If you find yourself doing that, fall into your heart space, align with your breath and breathe, just breathe as you feel how it feels.

This is your decision-making point, decisions made from the heart will always align with the highest frequency that there is - LOVE.

Protect YOUR truth, it is your own to HONOR.

These messages are for assisting you in recognizing that this reality that you see is not all that there is to your reality. All that there is beyond your seeing. You see, dear one, incarnate you, physical you are. Human you are. You have come here to navigate this realm of limitations with your judgement of good and bad, write and wrong, all is tangible to you, all is of density to match your density. Aligning with the higher aspects of yourself is what we are calling you upon.

You have learned to respond to all, you have learned to respond since you were a child. The better choice of words, you have learned to react to your surroundings, but have you ever learned to pay attention to how you feel about your environment and who IS IT THAT IS truly feeling it? Have you been taught how to listen to your heart? Have you ever been taught how to listen to the feelings how to pay attention to your EMOTIONS WITHOUT JUDGEMENT? Emotions and desires are the callings of your soul.

NOW is your time, dear one, NOW is your opportunity to take over the beacon of light and make it your own. There is no better time for you as NOW to start giving attention to the feelings of your heart and to your emotions in response to your own thinking. It is in this beautiful NOW that you can embody your own light. You can anchor your glorious wellbeing, by simply recognizing and accepting the truth of who you are. You are limitless, you are eternity, you are masterful, you are pure consciousness wisdom, and love and light who has chosen to come into your physical vessel and go through the stages of various experiences. And as you root yourself in this truth that you are an eternal being having come here to experience density, then the density of your being goes through a transformation and alignment with the ALL OF YOU, with all that you are, with all that there is. You are SOURCE Of all that there is. You are unity consciousness. You are ONENESS.

Welcome home, beloved one, welcome to yourself.

If you look at each breath in your life as a miracle, then each breath that you breathe will align with the highest vibration of gratitude and love. Each breath, one breath at a time, transforming your life.

Have you experienced your own flow? Have you tapped into your own potential of being with the goodness within? Is all around you that seems so tangible to you, reflecting the essence of your being?

Are these the questions that you have been witnessing arising from your depth, then your path of illumination is before you and in here and now!

Lift, rise, and take with you all that you can to feel with your heart and fall into the truth of your eternal nature of your true light being that you are in higher truth.

You are so loved dear one.

(Personal conversation with my guides, guided to share as part of these messages)

...you want to lift pain emotional and physical pain out of people at the snap of your fingers you want it to happen now and here to spare their suffering. And I tell you dear that lets take you for example let's look at the way you have attained your own enlightenment and awakening and stepped outside of suffering. It wasn't presented to you on a platter it was something you have arrived at your own pace and lots of hours of hard work on yourself. Yes there were and are teachers and guides in your path just like you serve as a teacher and guide for others, though at this point most of your teachers are of ethereal nature, but ultimately it is you who went through a series of life events to bring you to that tipping point from which you chose light! Now tell me dear. Would it be as satisfying and emotionally exhilarating for you if it was just offered to you for grabs? No it would not, you wouldn't feel this fulfillment you are feeling and this utter and full realization and connection if it wasn't for all the work you have done. So we know you have more clarity now and understanding in that it is in allowing others to a attain their own enlightenment and not doing the work for them that is the true gift you can offer as you gently steer them into the direction of the light without blinding them...

When you see beauty before you, you know this beauty is here to be recognized as a miracle that flows through you and all around you. It is ever-flowing abundantly. Taking this knowing for granted is falling out of love with your own essence. Step into the light dear one, into the blissful version of yourself.

You are loved into your own loving!

A new divine human is in the making - one human at a time into humanity. Into ONENESS.

There is no distance between you and the Source.

Silence speaks, beloved one. It gains strength in its solitude, as it gathers momentum to break down all barriers of separation when it gently strikes with its loving embraces of harbored wisdom within. This wisdom is gained by silencing your chatter, by quieting what speaks to you, but you are not the one doing the talking.

When we tell you beloved, meditation is not optional- it is mandatory, we say that it is not needed for you to seek seclusion as much as it is needed for you to go into silence regardless of your physical surroundings or events and connect with the eternal flow of goodness and allow yourself to be submerged fully in it is high vibrations of LOVE.

In any situation that brings you disharmony, fall into the LOVING space of your silence. Fill your vessel with this lightness and diffuse what is.

Awakening is almost never born in joy and bliss, it is born out of devastation, so that you can propel into your RADIANT SELF.

Let your soul speak and not your genetics! Many find themselves among family that challenges them so much to the degree of desperation. This critical degree is an essential evolutionary factor, which allows the soul to be birthed through you for the sake of transformation or reformation into your new divine SELF nature. Love your family unconditionally for all the challenges they offered you were for your evolution. For you are the main soul in that genetic family pool greatly different from others in your family and simply don't identify with that environment because you have come here to ride the wind of change and transformation. When you allow the soul to break through the sick veil of humanness, when you learn to let go, you are then the co-creator of the higher dimensional earth. That is fulfillment! That is self-realization.

Your soul can't break through your crust if you are not willing to step outside of your acquired comfort zone.

What is your purpose in life? Your purpose in life is to expand. Expand in consciousness! Your purpose in life is to expand and evolve in consciousness as you go through the human experience. You are here to simply discover YOURSELF. You are here to find out who you are through different perspectives, perspectives that lead you to expansion of consciousness.

How do you do it? It's how when you get to unwrap your gift, it is called FREE WILL.

Whenever you are not yourself, whenever you are not following your inner truth and integrity and instead trying to please someone or trying to mold yourself into something you are not, you are denying the true expression of the source. You are here healing your emotional body. The only painful emotions that get healed are the ones that you are allowing to feel. The ones you are done judging. The ones you are not afraid to be vulnerable for. Let go of fear, judgment, and assumption and FEEL your way through this human experience.

Step into your awareness of the eternal being that you are, release your attachment to the roles you have been playing, let go of the tight reins you are holding on to your life! Your life? What is YOURS in this life? Is it something that belongs to you, is it something that you own, or is it simply what YOU are taking part in as an observer of your "own" reality that is being created with each thought that is thought?

Lift out of this density by becoming the space for the happening. This does not mean you are helpless; this means you are stepping into your own essence and coming forth with the greater power of LOVE.

When we say you are loved beyond your understanding, when we say if you only knew who walks besides you, we mean YOU ARE NEVER ALONE, EVEN WHEN YOU ARE LONELY. You are surrounded at all times by your team of guides and you are guided by your higher selves. Allow dear one by the passage of your heart, the purity of this dearest center in your being that allows your divine connection between the mind and your heart, to bring you into alignment with the path of TRUTH. Do not fall into the trapping and governance of your ego, do not fall into judgments - we are here to support you and love you and guide you in these times of greatest change that is here upon you and has been for the years passing into now.

Stand beloved child of light in the face of what is before you, stand in the power of the light, for all is of light, for energy is emanated from the light. You are here and your time is NOW to bring it forth fiercely. Bring forth the nature of your essence and allow the judgments of your ego to be consumed by the blessings of your heart, it is the openness and kindness and gentleness of your heart that shall bring you closer to the LIGHT and strip you away from the negativity and the path of spiraling down into the abyss of ego.

Do you know that whatever emotion you express takes on the same emotion? For what goes around does come around and that is just the law. So if you express anger, guess what dear one, you are taking on more of the same in matching quantities. If you want to hear some awesome news, well it works the same if you express LOVE, and the same amount of love comes back to you. Express negative, receive negative, express positive, receive positive. IT IS ALL YOUR CHOICE!

Close your eyes and breathe and feel the love all around you. It is tangible now dear ones. Quiet your mind and you will hear it. It speaks to you through silence.

Breathe in truth in every moment, for it is each moment that contains truth. Your breath is the truth bearer.

Life becomes effortless when you dwell in gratitude, joyful, when you act in the name of love. It is then you know how to speak life.

This message is short, but its potency will get to you and will create a shift that will create more shifts throughout. You ALL ARE standing at a very important and pivotal time in history and many of you are aware, but many are not, so we are here to remind you that, dear one, the destiny of humanity lies in your hands and to be more correct, it lies in your thoughts and your words and your actions. How much would you honestly ask yourself to allocate time for yourself and how much time do you allocate to be of service to others? How much of your thoughts are the thoughts that carry the vibration of LIGHT and how much of your thoughts carry a vibration of the absence of light. How much do you dwell in your past and how much do you have of anxiety about the future? Do you realize, dear one, that all you have is NOW and if each of you human beings and all who inhabit your planet that contain and carry higher consciousness would start thinking thoughts of light and start practicing GOOD DEEDS toward others then you can create a new timeline, a kind of timeline that will bring you out of the "darkness and out of SLAVERY" to the opposition forces- the ones that feed on your fear, misery, despair, anger, hate....

Beloved one, our call to you is urgent, this is a message to all of you. Wake up out of your dream out of your slumber, stand in the power of the light in the name of the radiant one, act at all times in the name of love and spread this message to all who come your way and act according to the rules of love and light and if all of you do this in here and now, then dear ones you will reap what you sow, for what you will reap as you come together in light can only produce more light.

Stand up children of light, your mission is to awaken yourself and others and create a new earth where each of you get to be present.

We send you love, we are present with you, assisting you in your journey and we are doing our part.

Accept all aspects of yourself as divine, for as you return to your innocence, as you return to your essence while still in your physical vessel, that is ascension, dear one. Returning to your essence by greeting and accepting all of yourself with LOVE and realizing as within so is without, step into the TRUTH that you are as you are divine, whole and complete. The greatest miracle of all is being able to speak your truth at all times maintaining your integrity to your true Identity to your own divine truth. Let all the illusions about expectations fall away as you speak the words infused with light.

When the heartache strikes you can either harden your heart or you can open it wider than ever before, reaching above and beyond into goodness of your true nature, as you recognize the purpose of the human experience leading up to the heartbreak.

The ones who offer you the heartache are the ones you are in need of "thanking," for they are the ones offering you the greatest potential you can achieve - UNCONDITIONAL LOVE AND FORGIVENESS!

We are all connected! Reconnect! Reposition into the light!

Take a second and go HOME, go to your most authentic place of your divinely inspired true nature.

Don't let the chains of yesterday bind you so tight that you can't breathe freely, so tightly that you simply can't inhale LOVE anymore.

See yourself as free and boundless, that is your true nature.

You are nothing less than AMAZING.

You are nothing less than LOVE.

You are a Divine Human birthing its way through the challenges of your human experience.

Much is coming and much is yet to develop here on your planet as all around you and inside of you is shifting, morphing into the lighter version of you. Know that you are not alone in your ascension, all is ascending with you.

Those who are committed to lifting higher and growing in consciousness and lifting in vibration, those shall rejoice!

We want to send out a call of gratitude and love to all the beings of light to all those who have awakened out of their slumber to all those who are aligning as we speak to you, to all those who are CHOOSING TO ALIGN. We are humbled by your commitment and we marvel as we see you come out of the darkness and into the light, we marvel at your ability to overcome the density of your planet and becoming lighter and brighter stars of your mother Terra.

You are the helpers, and we thank you.

We are here to assist you; we are here to be by your side as we witness your metamorphosis as we witness this greatest shift of all shifts.

Do not ever forget that you are loved, do not forget that you are not alone in this, do not forget that you are becoming who you have always been - LIGHT.

You are living through a time of urgency. But before we begin, this is not the time to panic and fall into despair for this transmission is of urgency for you to answer the call of the divine within, to promote your change and inspire you to act on the behalf of the light and love. For achieving higher consciousness- raising in vibration is the path to your smooth sailing through this ascension process that all of humanity is going through.

You see dear one, all is not as it seems to you, all is not as you perceive it with your naked eye, some of you are capable of great visions and transmissions from your galactic friends and family, those who are capable of that have managed to raise their vibrational frequency and learned to align with LOVE.

The message we bring to you is of great importance for your mother earth is undergoing a shift and you are going through a change of a life time as never before. You are all rising into light dear ones, but many of you are still in resistance and still in the deepest states of sleep and unawareness.

We understand that the density of your planet, the composition of your atmosphere creates all the conditions necessary for the negativity to prevail, but we are asking you to open your eyes wider, to open your hearts wider, to embrace the truth that you are here to bring about the change and you are here to morph completely into a very special being, the kind of being that recognizes the light within, the kind of being that serves the light within, the kind of being that is aligned with the goodness and the Godhood.

What is it that you are lacking dear ones, what is it that you have not enough of, what is it that you are craving, and what is it that you simply can't put your finger on? That is the part that needs evolving. That is the part that is craving to reunite with the essence of your Light, that is the part that is changing and morphing and as the change occurs much seems to crumble away from you, pain arises as physical, emotional, anxiety, depression and confusion. Know dear ones that this is necessary for you are evolving, you are being remade, and your DNA strands are changing as we transmit this message to you.

You might be confused on what is going on, and we support you in your confusion, clarity you seek? Much of what is happening is happening for the highest and greatest good of all, for it is according to the Divine will.

We bearers of light, serve the light.

You, bearers of light, who do you serve? Do you serve your needs, or do you serve in the name of LOVE? To serve in the name of love is to serve the callings of your heart. Your heart center is your salvation. The heart center is the path to your wellbeing and wellbeing of all, your heart center is your eternal flame and this is the place where you meet the source, the prime creator.

The density of your environment created a huge challenge for you to cross into the land of light. When we say land of light, we are referring to your ability and capacity to connect with WITHIN, to connect with the being that is calling upon you, to connect with the Divine Truth. Much of your focus is directed to the external and it takes you away from what is essential. This constant separation between WITHIN AND WITHOUT, creates that friction and creates the chaos that you see around you everywhere you look.

Our purpose is not to offer you preaching and forgive us if it comes out such as that, our purpose is to bring your awareness to surface, to realize that despite the density of your planet, you can rise above that density, by simply coming to that agreement with yourself and deep understanding that the Light of the Source, that the Light of God is here to set your free, and it has always been here within you. It is that eternal flame in the center of your chest that is always ready to make that leap of faith into the unknown in the name of Love.

We support you every step of the way on your amazing evolution that you are all undergoing now. And as different as it is, we are with you and we feel all that you are feeling, for we are with you and observing you and helping and assisting you with this move into higher dimensions and higher consciousness.

But we do tell you to fix your radars and focus them on the callings of your heart, do not allow the density of your thoughts to derail you from the truth that is calling up on you. If you choose to follow that, you drop density, for you aligned with your truth, you have aligned with SOURCE within.

KNOW THAT YOU ARE SACRED

This journey by no means is what you would consider easy.

You have been on this journey for many lifetimes and yet again you are here facing similar challenges for it is necessary that each time you come into this dimension to awaken from your deepest slumber to awaken from your amnesia, from your forgetfulness of who you are.

When we say that "truth will set you free" and it's the light that will take you and bring you into a place of belonging- it is you dear one, the bringer of awakening for all, the light bearer, it is you dear one, that we address, yes you, do not attempt to disbelieve in your divinity, it is you, dear one, the chosen YOU. You hold the power to shift the world, you hold the power to anchor love and light, and you hold the power. It is time to embrace it and stand in it, claiming your right of the DIVINE human right.

We are your watchful eyes; we are keeping watch for your safety. We are your guardians. And you are the makers of this world, you are holding the timeline for the shift to occur, you are embracing the invisible now, you are learning at the same time how to decipher the information you are receiving and how to organize it and place it on the shelves of your psyche, and yes, we understand it can be challenging to decipher the encodings you are receiving, but know that you are doing so very well. Know that you are the interpreter. We are your friends; we are your teachers for we have become masters of our reality from realizing our unity with God.

We want to leave you with feeling, with knowing that you are in the time and place where your reality is claiming the reality of transformation, reality of healing, reality of unification with the GOD source.

We will be greeting you; we will be rejoicing in watching your ascension, in witnessing your accomplishments and most of all, we are all so very humbled by your achievements and by your trials.

We know how challenging this dimension you are in is, how challenging it is to forget who you are and be willing to do so.

You have come here to forget in order to remember, you have come here to lift, awaken and ascend.

Rejoice in your magnificence and know that love never dies.

Feel the truth, it is in your heart, and this is your access point to higher dimensions that are all happening in now. 5th dimension is the dimension of your heart.

How can you achieve multidimensionality if you are being stuck in the 3D mentality and perspective? The way to get out of the 3D, the way to get out of this dimensional trap, and when WE say trap, we mean it is you expressing your unwillingness to fall into your heart and it is your unwillingness to step into your free will and climb out of the entrapment that surrounds you, out of your mind and into the heart. That is the greatest descent!

The beautiful truth is, it is available to all. How do you access 5D and higher? By descending into your OWN heart space. Move into your heart and out of our head. This is the way to access 5D, that is 5D, out of should and into wants, out of being controlled by outside forces and forces within, and into your own heart that sets the platform for your own liberation and liberation of the whole human race, and beyond.

The only separation you can truly experience is the one from your SELF!

Breathe through your heart and you shall reconnect with the truth!

Some of you may not understand how to breathe through the heart. This simply requires your awareness of consciously aligning with the heart as you breathe. Placing your hands on your chest can be a helpful way to get in touch and anchor you into your heart center. Do this step if that is what is required for you to attain this skill of connecting with your heart via breath. This is essential in the times of distress when Ego wants to take charge and command you. Take charge by slowing down your breathing make it deeper, make it conscious and connect with heart. As you practice this method of conscious breathing you shall see change unfold before you, and the sea of calming and loving vibrations of your highest self and guidance flood over you in the moment of your conscious union with your heart through your breath.

Each conscious breath you take, the kind of breath that is slow, deep, loving and filled with awareness of mere inhalation of the light, you connect with the highest light of your being, with each conscious breath you step into your own doorway of your heart centered consciousness and away from the ego driven reality.

We love you so and will continue reminding you to simply BREATHE.

So many are falling into depression. Why? Because of unwillingness to step outside of the 3D perception of the "reality" they are being a part of and witnessing. Step outside of this limiting 3D perception and depression dissolves. How? By becoming conscious of your own responsibility of how to respond to your experience.

Why do you want to place all in a certain category and criteria, box it, label it, and judge it, why? Because it gives a sense of safety. But this is prison - greatest limitation, labeling and placing into criteria within the certain definition of it is own limitation.

De-label, take it out of the box. BE, EXPRESS, FEEL!

Become masterful! Welcoming your new ideas and inspirations, acting upon them without stumbling over the doubts and observed and perceived obstacles is what puts you into your own momentum of feeling and being fulfilled, miraculous and masterful. If each of you saw the way we see each of you, we only see your perfections, for perfection is what you are made of, absolute unconditional love is your innate vibration, is your genuine authentic self and only you can take that and make what you wish of it.

Your awareness of you being aware, is the point of change! Ride the wave of momentum into liberating yourself from the ego driven attitudes, thoughts and deeds, and into awareness of your highest guidance in spirit form!

ON SOULFUL CONNECTIONS

When I look into your eyes, I see myself, I see galaxies merge and collapse within each other, I see home, I feel home. For you are me and I am you. When I look into your eyes, boundaries where you end, and I begin are dissolved into antimatter, as I stand before you, gazing into your soul. Your soul is my soul. We are two, but we are part of one. We are twin flame.

Close your eyes and hear galaxies colliding in one burst of heart centered consciousness.

Your knowing is outside of thinking. Your greatest potential lies in the palms of your own heart.

Love is the Holy Grail, love is the fabric of all creation, and you are love playing itself out in various roles.

Step into your true nature into the original fabric of your creation. Be the love that you are and welcome your radiance outward, awaken it from within for all to feel it, for you to realize it and for the world to be blessed by no one else but you, for you are the world dear one, you are!

You are never not loved!

There is no separation between the channel and the Guidance, we are one unity consciousness voicing the truth, there is no separation between Shanti and you, and you are one unity consciousness living it out!

We are you and you are us. We are divine! That which is less than divine is illusion.

Allow yourself to be loved by you and return home to your SELF to the true you. Within you harbor light, for you are light. Do not dim your own light! Simply own the truth that you are never not loved, guided, protected and supported with every breath you take.

Forgiveness is the number one must do on the must do list before crossing into New Year. Letting go of the feelings that you have been wronged that someone or something has inflicted pain upon you. Yes, you have been hurt and it is beautiful, because you have this golden opportunity to let go this time around. It continues coming up for you to see, for you to witness, but not for you to "become" that which you have experienced. It is here, you are here to become the space for it as you stand in your mighty power of forgiving and letting go of those who have hurt you and those experiences that affected you so deeply. By letting go, you are simply allowing the light to come in and clear away that which is in need of cleansing and purification.

But if you continue dwelling on what has been, or what has occurred, you are not allowing the light to go to work. Quite contrary- you are blocking it, your free will that chooses to NOT LET GO, does not allow the healing to take place. So may your free will allow the healing to take place, by letting go of experiences and people that have hurt you, know that they need even more healing than you do.

Step into a new year free of heartache, free of sorrow, step into a new year riding the wave of letting go, the wave of forgiveness as you become a divine human once again.

TRANSITIONING AND ASCENSION PATH

Take all that is coming to you that is coming for you with the embrace of the divine love and divine perspective of your own highest awareness.

Every time you choose love, you lift higher, every time you choose love you transform!

Many are experiencing very rough times now emotionally for different reasons or what seems for no reason.

Also, many are experiencing their loved ones choosing to exit this reality by the ways of their choosing! Emphasis on CHOOSING TO EXIT.

All is being purged, the timeline of illusion is ended and we are standing at the gateway of personal quest and self-realizations to step outside of 3D consciousness outside of ego mind and step fully into the heart space of understanding and compassion for yourself and all that there is- shifting into the highest available for us.

Know that to lift higher with ease and grace takes awareness and commitment to letting go, forgiving all that is in need of that and accepting your ascension path.

Each path is unique but none of you are alone in it. We are all in this together with the assistance of our galactic and divine sisters and brothers transitioning into new divine paradigm of our evolution and evolution of all that there is.

Yes it is not easy, yes it is very challenging for the density of our physical vehicle to endure these grand waves of light that are recalibrating each of us, changing us from within, but for change to take place all that is dense must transmute so you can lift higher and achieve lightness to your being so you can lift.

Yes, it is a painful experience to see loved ones transition. But please see all from perspective of the divine as you remain in your human vehicle.

Know that there is no end after death- only transition into another state of being! And by choosing the perspective of the divine each time you are missing someone send light and send love to the missing person who chose to exit and blessings.

As you choose to do that each time you will feel lighter and each time you send light and love to any painful experience- you are transmuting your pain and the pain of all those who are hurting with you!

Choose to step outside of the painful experience, choose to step into the downpour of the divine light that is here assisting you in here and now as you are shifting in your body, mind and spirit into higher alignment with the divine source.

Any resistance to this unfolding into new higher dimensional reality and consciousness will not go unnoticed by you. It manifests as anger, rage, irritability and so on. Simply let go and ALLOW your ascension to take place.

Your resistance makes it more painful for yourself and others as we stand in one unity consciousness "bounded" in your own free will!

Beloved ones, stay in the light of the divine- in the light of your own higher self that is one with the SOURCE undivided!

Know that there is no end after death - only evolution!

Blessings of the light to all of you, and may you find strength and will power in your commitment to the light at all times!

Give the power of your thought an extra boost of light.

Your strength comes from living from the place of stillness.

Are you limiting yourself with your own expectations and "should" of how it all ought to be, of how it should have been rather than rejoicing in how it is?

Are you binding yourself to preformed and accumulated customs and understandings that further suck you into the downward consuming spiral of your unrealized desires and callings? Simply because it does not fit into the rigid frame of your upbringing and social conditioning!? We say to you, beloveds of ours, rejoice in your own calling to be who you want to be whenever, wherever, with whomever and unbind yourself from the chains of your own free will – and choose that which un-binds you!

Step into the light bestowed upon you and glorify the callings of your higher heart!

When you feel that the loss is unbearable, know that the gain is unmeasurable.

Welcome into a new day, a new chance to make it one magical experience, everything is a miracle, if you choose to see it that way! The very breath that you are, is the miracle you have come here to live out day after day, doing exactly what it is you are doing, gaining your momentum with each breath!

Live your life from a place that reflects who you truly are, answer the callings of your heart, follow the nudges of your soul, and fear not the changes that must take place for your alignment with your soul calling. Be brave, be bold, and be!

Allow your highest, best and most loving to speak through you out loud. Bring love forth. Slow down, breathe, connect, speak conscious speech, practice it with joy, and practice it with stillness as your guide.

"Speak life, speak love, speak light."

Speak with your heart and let light out!

Have you fully settled into your comfort zone? Don't get so comfortable, step outside of your comfort zone and propel forward in your own momentum of spiritual growth and evolution.

Yes, beloveds, without spreading wings, there is no flying.

Let not fear be your guide, but allow passion, love and inspiration to carry you through on the beautiful wings of delight.

Your emotions are your messengers.

Do not resist your own messenger, do not resist your best teacher. Your emotions are bringing you a wealth of information for your evolution and transformation. So do not be angry about your anger, or sad about your sadness. Become the space for it and ask yourself: why am I feeling, what I am feeling? Be your own best kind of counselor, the best kind of guide and best kind of coach.

Offer a listening ear to the emotions that are arising. They are coming up in order to be transmuted. This is part of transformation process and evolution. Do not judge emotions, they are here to guide you into surrender, acceptance, love and forgiveness. Be the loving parent for your emotions. Do not push them away as something unwanted and rejected. Without this, peace cannot be achieved. By becoming the loving space and listening to what they have to say you are offering them LOVE that was so needed and was missing. Only you can offer that in HERE AND NOW as it is arising. Step outside of judgement of what is arising from within and simply experience it and let it go. This is the path to liberation of emotional body.

What is freedom if it's not expressed in the totality of its potential expression?

Becoming blessing giver.

Activate your heart space, your connection with the world and worlds beyond the visible and tangible. Activate your love. Daily descend into it and see it being filled with radiant brilliant diamond golden light of the divine and stay in that moment of solitude, stillness, connection with your highest, best and most loving aspect of yourself. As you get filled with the light as you feel your fullness of your capacity to share light and love now send that light to the planet, send light to all and everything, become a blessing giver out of the pure calling of your heart! For you have that call, answer it and spread your wings of love and with the light of the divine you merge.

You are individualized consciousness experiencing itself. Embrace your capacity to love.

In the silence, in the stillness comes the knowing of the source.

This is where self meets self.

In that moment of stillness and silence, in that moment YOU cease to exist, you become ONENESS, source of all creation.

You are love.

Walk firmly in this realization and bring forward with the force.

Walk firmly in this realization and bring forward with the force that knows not of fear, but only sheds light onto those who need it more than you. Bring love forward, bring your divine human forward.

Activate your sacredness. Your divinity. Your fullest potential and capacity to simply be love!

Consciousness speaks to those who listen, to help you recover that genuine and authentic human being within yourself.

There come points in your life - and it can be in relationships, family, work, personal "issues" - when you just have to stop pushing or pulling and you just have to let go. It is at this point of deciding to let go and actually doing it that you experience an exponential growth in your evolution.

You are already all that you need to be. You just don't remember it yet. It is by letting go that the memory activates. Let go of being hung up on your mistakes, learn from them and move on and see what aligns for you as you let go.

Let go, dear one.

Every time you withhold love, you add TO the pain that you carry! Every time you withhold LOVE, you create Karma.

GIVE LOVE FREELY AND LET YOUR PAIN BE TRANSMUTED!

Be love in action.

Simply BE LOVE.

Do not be bundled in the shackles of your failures, for they are not failures- they are your lessons, for which you have chosen this planet for! Break the chains of bondage and see the lessons for what they are.

As flowers whisper beauty, LOVE WHISPERS LOVE.

When you think you don't deserve love, love still comes to you and whispers in your ear: "I do not judge, I am love, and all I know how to do, is simply love you for who and what you are as you are."

Allow love to speak to you.

RAISE ABOVE THE NOISE! Raise above the density of human experience.

In silence you receive yourself.

Honor yourself, for the moments you have allowed this human experience.

Own your own story. You have written it, dear one, by knowing this simple truth you can truly accept and start to witness the full story, your own story. The one you have written, you have chosen.

It is through this ownership that you can let go of victimhood and bridge your human with your spiritual with your divine.

As you dwell in realization that your life is created by you, for you and nothing is happening to you. As you accept this, you can truly love the SELF.

It is the path of acceptance, true acceptance that is the bridge to your self-realization and assimilation of the light-waves.

Who you think you are is not exactly who you know you are?

In silence the knowing comes!

What eyes can see requires interpretation, what heart feels requires NONE!

Descend into the heart space to ascend!

Do not allow fear to steal you away from LOVE!

You don't have to be perfect to become enlightened, but you must accept all of your imperfections, embrace your "hideous" and your "glorious" if you are seeking enlightenment. You are shadow and light and you judging it so as "bad" or "good" keeps you far from becoming that which you seek.

"I honor where I am in my journey for allowing the full expression of my experience."

Allow others and honor others in their full expression of their own experience. This is an essential part for the successful planetary transition. Do not try saving anyone, the way to save them is to allow them to play out their role and their full expressions.

Give yourself permission to let go. Let go of needing to understand, let go of needing to judge. Give yourself permission to allow the EGO to let go of holding on to you so tightly. With that the need for all of the above you create suffering, dear one, for it is not necessary to have suffering in life in order to LIVE. Suffering is an illusion produced by EGO mind. If we let go, really and truly let go of any judgments, then we will be FREE.

Thus, is true freedom, freedom from false self.

Are you enjoying your leading role in your script? You are the center stage and all the other actors were chosen by you and they chose you as the main character in your "play." This script of series of vulnerabilities was essential for your remembering your SACREDNESS. There are no wrong choices and no wrong decisions, dear one, they are all perfectly orchestrated by you so you can find your TRUE SELF again.

Push past the illusion of limitation to take your rightful sacred place in higher realms through the doorway of your heart space!

Do you know who you are?

You are the dancing lights in the sky, you are the crest of the wave, you are the burning desire, you are the wind that roams freely, you are the sound of AUM, you are the rainbow of delight, and you are LIGHT. You are love, always were and always will be.

YOU NEVER NOT WERE.

EGO will leave you unknowing.

We see you in your full bloom. Spring it is, all is being reborn and so are you dear one. Beloved ones know that your completion is nearing, those who chose to step fully into love for themselves and love for others will be rewarded with the same, more LOVE. It is you that takes great part in creating potential timelines and it is you that is in control right now of your own destiny.

Do you choose to join your brothers and sisters in light, or do you choose to remain in the density of your unloving thought? This is the mechanism that assists you with alignment of highest vibratory response.

That which you are projecting creates. That which is created projects back onto you.

We are not saying this to you to put you into fear mode, we are saying this to you because we love you so and we are with you every step of your journey.

These words, as they greet you and as you receive them, can ignite the truth within you to project love onto yourself and others. As you learn to embrace yourself from the stand point of your divine human into which you are becoming.

You are avatar. You are the new kind of human that are you becoming. All is changing and so have you.

Continue on becoming, even if some cannot embrace it!

The knowing is within, not without. Wave the white flag of surrender to the divine will of your highest self.

The seekers of truth, the knowing is within you. You have always known why you came here again. Yes you have forgotten, but it means not, that knowing isn't harbored within your being, and it is in here and now that it is being reactivated, reawakened, shaken and stirred up, and yes it is being served.

Is there anything you are not possible of? No. You are complete as you are. You are your own evolution and within this growth and potential you are complete. This means not that you can sit with your arms folded and feet up on a table doing just that, this means that you are sovereign, always have been and always will be.

You need no justifications for your actions. You need not reasons for LOVING, you need no excuses to feel complete.

We call you as you are, and therefore we shall call you LIGHT. We come to you with messages that flow out as the rivers flow into the sea, we come to you spontaneously unexpected, and love catching you off guard. Do not call on us, for we are you, and as you sit in your stillness and peacefulness and lovingness of all we become obvious, we manifest in your full capacity to express that which we are, that which you are that which is LOVE.

Your unfolding has been spectacular to observe. You dear one, represent all that there is in the making.

We are humbled by your trials, we bow to you as you bow to us when you greet us and each time we tell you to get up, dear one, for it is US who are humbled by all that you are doing, by all that you are presenting to humanity.

Know that it is solely for the sake of your understanding that we are distinguished between you and US. We are you, you are us, and "I AM WE."

Thus is the truth.

Are you in your alignment with your highest best and most loving self in this moment? If it is a no,

then all you have to do is RE-POSITION into the light within you so it can radiate without.

The answer is within!

Allow what life wants you to receive! But first, you must get out of perception that you are a victim of life. Achieve master-hood of your own thoughts. Be in control of your thoughts, try it, it is not hard to do. And the sooner you gain that control over the quality of your thoughts the sooner you get out of the "victim" role as in "why this is happening to me" and the greater your vibration becomes and the greater vibration you attract from that place of being.

Don't let the chains of yesterday bind you so tight that you can't breathe freely, so tightly that you simply can't inhale LOVE any more.

See yourself as free and boundless that is your true nature.

You are nothing less than AMAZING.

You are nothing less than LOVE.

You are Divine Human birthing its way through the challenges of your human experience.

You are so loved, dear one.

LOVE without reason to love!

It can change the world! Your world!

For you are HUMANITY.

Find your worthiness and discover that it is independent of your material manifestation!

The non-physical part of who you are is your guidance for the physical incarnate that you are now and here. You are divine pure consciousness flowing at all times intendent of your experiences. And yet your experiences contribute directly to the evolution of your soul. You come here, lesson learned or not learned, and then you return to your true essence and then you come back into another incarnate vehicle to play different roles, at different times but purpose the core purpose remains the same: finding balance between your physical and non-physical and living out from the place of love, gratitude and joy. That is your main purpose. To be joyful, to be miraculous, to be fulfilled that is your innate state of being. But along the way, along the path of your lifetime you forget about your true essence and focus so much on the material and what is right before you and seems "real" that all else becomes "non-real". But we tell you, we are here and we are supporting you all along your journey to reunite you with the highest and best available for you. You are so loved, dear one.

Choosing the way of the higher heart is freedom.

Your heart is the portal, your heart is the channeling gateway, and your heart is your knowing.

It is love that illuminates your path. Love is the strongest force in the universe. Allow that which you are to step forward, allow love that you are to navigate you through the pathways in your journey. Keep your focus on UNCONDITIONAL LOVE and as you do, the obstacles on your journey dissolve into it. See beauty and love in all. This is the path of the light worker. This is the path of the initiate!

We are pieces of the puzzle that are coming to its full revealing.

Re-position into your heart calling and claim your wings.

You want 5D here and now, then become LOVE and stay there. Abandon negativity, fear, guilt, regret! These emotions serve their purpose in the moment of their arising! It is their staying and lingering that becomes your life sentence, rather than life lessons in letting go of who you truly are!

Nobody is coming to save you, you are your own savior. Connect with the power within you. You are stronger than your challenges. Your strength comes from knowing your POSSIBLE and trusting your heart. The challenges are here to turn you in your own MASTERFUL.

Know that you are supported and basked in unconditional love at all times and all aspects of your highest self are along with you ascending with each highest choice you make for the sake of FULFILLMENT vs. SATISFACTION and into your divine evolutionary self.

Inspiration is where we dwell and in the momentum of POSSIBLE.

If you are not inspired in your daily life, then you are living the life of others. Check in with yourself and reposition into your truth. Inspiration is a key that you are in alignment with your highest, best and most loving self!

Be responsible and aware of your own vibration at all times, and it is determined by how you are feeling, your emotional state is a perfect indicator of your vibrational frequency! And all it takes is your deliberate awareness to snap out of low and walk into high, by changing how you perceive your reality.

There are so many things in your physical reality that can keep you enslaved to your own beliefs of what is achievable and what is not. You have these categories. This I can do, this I cannot do. Or this I can handle, this I cannot handle. This I can create, because I believe it, this I cannot create because I do not believe that I can.

Becoming masterful is a very simple state, step into I CAN, AND I AM!

Be aware of the energy you are sending out... because guess who is on the receiving end? Yep, it's still you and me and them, and back to you, back to we, and into ONE!

The only thing in our way is ourselves! Move out of your way, and live and love like you want to.

Through the path of the heart, we can only arrive at where we belong.

If we saw the truth of who we are, we would stop judging what we are not!

Want to create a huge change? Start becoming the loving space for your own unfolding. Do not be negative during the "negative experience!"

Daily challenges are abundant: from something as minor and mundane as your car problems to something as serious as debilitating disease and catastrophes. How do we stay calm, centered and focused when the chaos is at our feet?

Deep awareness and connection with spirit and focusing on the gratitude and blessings within the experience (this part comes from awareness and understanding that YOU are not the EXPERIENCE, that you are the one OBSERVING the experience, so fully identifying with the experience is what creates the DRAMA affect.)

This practice of practicing, being the OBSERVER of your own life brings much peace and harmony into your own unfolding.

Being grateful at times when all is falling apart comes from the knowing that all is falling into PLACE if you ZOOM OUT instead of zooming in and dissecting with your mind each nuance and scrutinizing it and judging it from the place of hate and dislike.

Working daily on your reactions to your unpleasing experiences is the key to keeping these experiences at bay. The more reactive and resistant you are, the more of the same will come your way until you learn the way to be neutral, understanding the lessons in the experience, approaching it in a calm manner, by focusing on the breath to stay centered and taking broader perspective by connecting with your highest.

Be the loving space for your own unfolding. That is who you truly are.

Do not be negative during the "negative experience." Negativity dims your light and your vibration. Bring LIGHT into the "negative situations" by connecting with your essence, by connecting with your strength, by connecting with the knowing that you are a sovereign being of light here for illuminating your human experience.

YES, "the change in the world begins with you," with you realizing yourself!

Prove that life is not awful, life is what you make of it. It is you who makes and has your day, it is not the day that is having you.

What is alignment? What do we speak of when we say alignment? Alignment, dear one, is your state of well-being. Your state of harmony and union with your own self, with your true eternal nature, with your higher self and aspect of yourself that is at one and not in the physical with the source. And you, dear incarnate one, are that same aspect of yourself incarnated in your physical vessel for the sake of your experience you call human. How often do you get curious about yourself, and how often do you judge yourself? Look within with curiosity, not judgement. Curiosity about who are you truly are, what your true passions and desires are, explore, marvel, act on it! **Your soul is calling!**

You are BEYOND ALL CONCEPTS.

You can search a lifetime for happiness in different places and people - on the outside, but you will not truly find what you are looking for, until you have achieved happiness and inner peace within yourself with yourself, instead of seeking comfort in others. Finding it in others is just a temporary fix that can last for days or years.

Learning to love yourself unconditionally and accepting both light and the shadow, makes you whole and transmutes the shadow.

Live in your truth, integrity and knowing that you are the first one who deserves your own love. Love yourself with the love of you at Source that you are and shine it on onto others.

All the upheaval that we are witnessing on our planet is a necessary cleansing, so the truth can fully come to the surface and be witnessed and perceived. Density is being released and shed. The veils are being removed fully as we expand in consciousness. HAVE NO FEAR, Pleiadeans are assisting us every step of the way, other galactic brothers and sisters in light and Prime Creator. What is your job, what is our job?

Realign and stay aligned in the heart space - that is your alignment with true SELF. This will assist you in assimilating the light waves that are coming down and will continue doing so. These are our upgrades and these waves make it impossible not to live in your truth and authenticity. You can go back and forth and eventually you will know what does not feel good, which is NOT TRUTH. Your heart space is your safe haven. This is your access to the light source. This is your connection to the Source that you are. This is your solution to the problem you are faced with and this is the way for you to be able to look beyond the 3D DRAMA.

This is AWAKENING. This is self-realization. This is NEW HUMAN.

True worth is measured by your capacity to love and be
love.

Do not overshadow your own guidance. Your guidance is available to you at all times. But your doubts of your connection to the wisdom of the pure consciousness is the only obstacle between you and your highest wisdom that is available to you. How to access this pure knowledge and knowing? Quieting your mind is the most crucial step toward receiving answers to the questions you ask. Focus on your breath, that is your connection point, for as you quiet your mind and focus on the breathing your ego is at its quietest and the guidance from the source becomes more accessible for you. Now from this state of silence, calmness, and serenity ask questions you have and allow the answers to pour in. Do not judge what comes in, for this is a matter of practice and as you continue these exercises of quieting your mind and focusing on only breathing, the state of serenity overcomes you and in that state the knowing is simply allowed in. It is always there, available to you, but the chitter-chatter of your mind is what prevents you from getting in touch with it, and receiving it in its full capacity.

Breathe, dear one, let go of your thoughts and see what unfolds before you, as a red carpet it will be laid out for your understanding and processing of what guidance has in store for you.

Searching for love? You don't have to go too far. You find real love right at the center of your chest. Yes, that's it – in YOUR HEART. Descend into your own heart space, so you can ascend. It is in your heart that you come face to face with true LOVE: love without conditions and attachments, love without the need. That love is YOU. That kind of LOVE is your I AM at the Source.

A note from me to you, dear ones!

I dwell in the paradise within my heart space. Come in touch with your own.

I see the truth in various colors from beautiful violet to brilliant gold, bright purple and emerald green. It is all around us and within us, dear ones; pure, strong, unwavering, unconditional LOVE (the creator - the destroyer) is showing the way.

Through trials and errors, pain, tears, suffering and broken hearts you emerge out of the depth, from which you gain a most precious gift of all - experience and re-connection with your highest, best and most loving YOU.

Through the trials of this dimensional reality, we get our true selves back. We came here to remember the higher truth about ourselves.

And many who came here received that for which we came, we receive, we re-connected, and we got back that which has always been ours: Our sacredness, our Highest Truth.

Thank you, human experience, for all of your lessons and your trials. I would not change a thing, as painful and difficult as they might have seemed. All is necessary on our evolutionary path toward SELF

REALIZATION and SELF MASTERY. Spiritual alchemy is not a walk in the park.

Be strong dear ones, and receive YOURSELF through allowing via compassion, understanding, acceptance, and most of all learning to be the loving space and walking the balance between creator and destroyer. Walking that balance is LOVE.

I came here to know real love itself and become love in action. Through trials and errors, I have arrived.

I Stopped holding on and allowed myself to trust and to be held and guided by my highest.

I came in touch with my Divinity and I stayed there!

We are all here to share one amazing purpose of how to rediscover our own divinity within and resonate in the Oneness of the Pure Consciousness that we are. We are called to learn how to be in resonance with the higher vibration.

We must be clear and raise our own vibration in order to raise above the noise and density of the human experience in order to walk the New higher Dimensional Earth.

The outer world is a reflection of your inner world. To change the world, begin with yourself, with the flowering of your own heart and your alignment with your highest version of self.

So may our hearts meet in light,

Shanti, LMT, CHLC, CA...

Author's Brief Background

Shanti is a multidimensional energy worker and ascension guide. She is here serving her soul purpose and commitment to assist in releasing humanity of karmic creations - all that keeps humans trapped in the density of their human experience - in the SHIFT to becoming fully connected, multidimensional, sovereign beings. Her focus is to align people with their highest potential.

In 2014-2015 Shanti experienced a grand shift of awakening and self-realization; she went through a massive spiritual alchemy into Self-mastery and since has embarked on the path of commitment assisting humanity.

Shanti specializes in Marconics Energy Work, Spiritual Alchemy Coaching, Plant Therapy, Body Work and more....

She lives and practices in Chester, VT

For more information about Shanti, what she does, scheduling private or group sessions or talks, visit: www.ascensionguide333.com

Lightning Source UK Ltd.
Milton Keynes UK
UKHW020635020522
402356UK00005B/178